DATE DUE

DEMCO 38-296

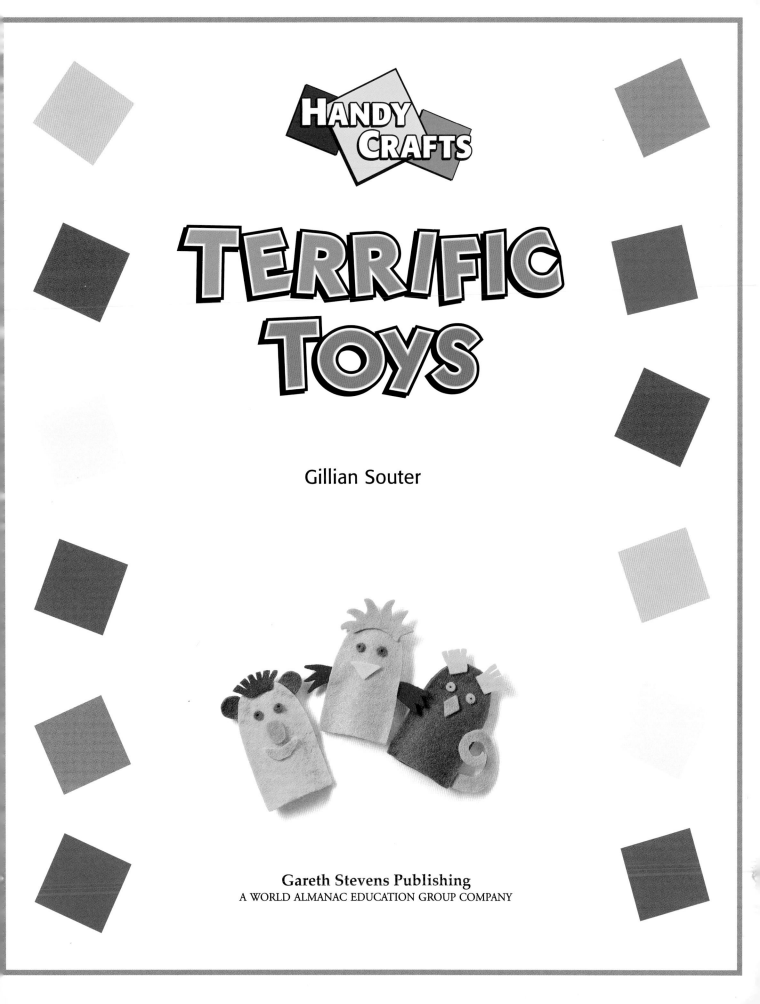

Handy Crafts

TERRIFIC TOYS

Gillian Souter

Gareth Stevens Publishing
A WORLD ALMANAC EDUCATION GROUP COMPANY

✦ Before You Start ✦

Some of these projects can get messy, so make sure your work area is covered with newspaper. For projects that need paint, you can use acrylic paint, poster paint, or any other kind of paint that is labeled nontoxic. Ask an adult to help you find paints that are safe to use. You will also need an adult's help to make some of the projects, especially when you have to stitch fabric, poke holes with pointed objects, use a craft knife or any other sharp cutting utensils, or bake something in an oven.

Please visit our web site at: www.garethstevens.com
For a free color catalog describing Gareth Stevens Publishing's list of high-quality books and multimedia programs, call 1-800-542-2595 or fax your request to (414) 332-3567.

Library of Congress Cataloging-in-Publication Data

Souter, Gillian.
    Terrific toys / by Gillian Souter.
       p. cm. — (Handy crafts)
    Includes bibliographical references and index.
    Summary: Provides instructions for making a variety of simple toys, including spinners, pickup sticks, parachutes, cork boats, juggling blocks, bead dolls, and more.
    ISBN 0-8368-3053-9 (lib. bdg.)
    1. Toy making—Juvenile literature. [1. Toy making. 2. Handicraft.] I. Title. II. Series.
TT174.S57   2002
745.592—dc21   2001055098

This edition first published in 2002 by
Gareth Stevens Publishing
A World Almanac Education Group Company
330 West Olive Street, Suite 100
Milwaukee, Wisconsin 53212 USA

This U.S. edition © 2002 by Gareth Stevens, Inc. Original edition published as *Games and Toys* in 2000 by Off the Shelf Publishing, 32 Thomas Street, Lewisham NSW 2049, Australia. Projects, text, and layout © 2000 by Off the Shelf Publishing. Additional end matter © 2002 by Gareth Stevens, Inc.

Illustrations: Clare Watson
Photographs: Andre Martin
Cover design: Joel Bucaro and Scott M. Krall
Gareth Stevens editor: JoAnn Early Macken

Printed in the United States of America

1 2 3 4 5 6 7 8 9 06 05 04 03 02

Contents

The Right Stuff

Most of the things you'll need to make terrific toys and games can be found around the house.

Different types of paper and cardboard are basic materials to keep on hand. You can buy sheets of paper and cardboard in many bright colors, but save empty cereal boxes and old greeting cards, too.

A good set of markers will be useful for many projects. Get washable markers to keep your clothes nice!

You can buy squares of colored felt at craft shops. Keep any leftover scraps of felt for future projects.

Several projects in this book use drinking straws or ice cream sticks. You can collect ice cream sticks or buy a package of them at a craft store.

Keep cardboard tubes, in all sizes, from toilet paper, paper towels, wrapping paper, and plastic wrap. Empty matchboxes and plastic bottles are also very useful.

Buttons, beads, and beans all make ideal playing pieces for board games.

Tops and Spinners

Make a colorful top to twirl — or spin a number to play a game!

You Will Need

- compass
- pencil
- stiff cardboard
- scissors
- markers
- toothpicks
- ruler

1 For a spinning top, use a compass to draw a circle on a piece of stiff cardboard.

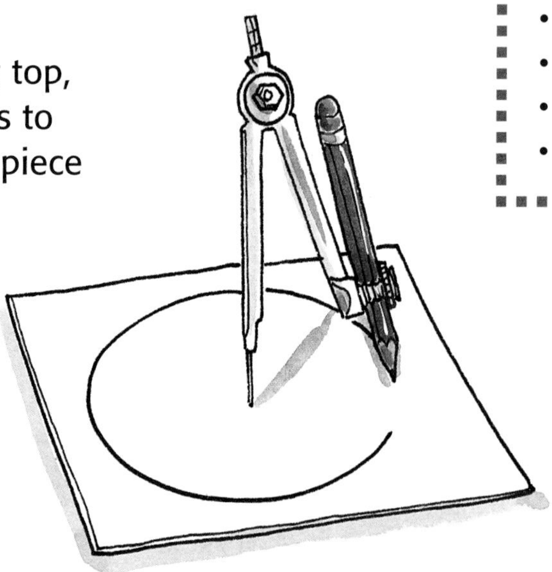

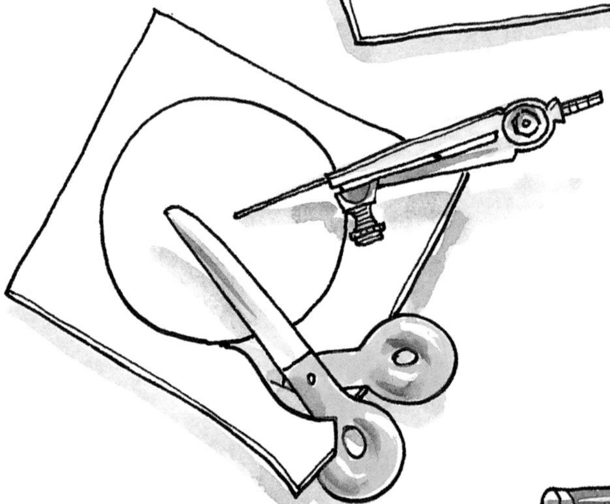

2 Carefully poke a hole in the center of the cardboard circle with the point of the compass. Cut out the circle.

3 Decorate the circle with markers. Push a toothpick into the hole, stopping two-thirds of the way through.

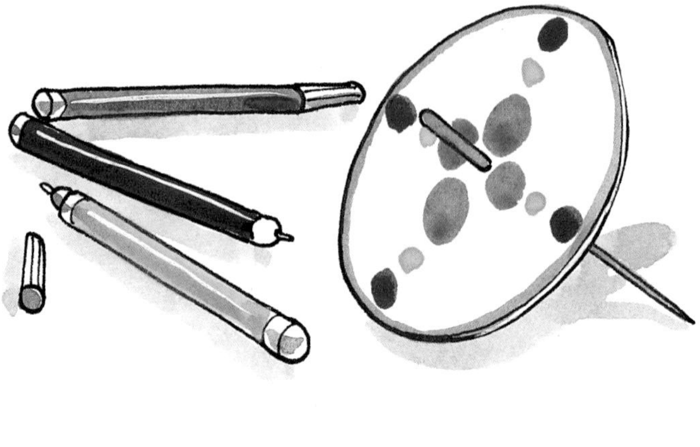

4 To make a spinner, draw a circle with a compass. Then draw lines to divide the circle into six equal sections.

5 Draw more lines to join the dividing lines. Cut along the outside lines to make a hexagon. Follow step 2 (page 6) to poke a hole in the center. Then follow step 3.

★ Bright Idea ★
Decorate your top with two lines of colored dots that cross in the center of the circle (see right). When you spin the top, the dots will look like bands of color.

★ Helpful Hint ★
To use your spinner, instead of dice, for a board game, draw a number from 1 to 6 in each section.

Remember This?

Test your memory with a matching pictures game. Just find two of a kind!

1 Cover one side of a sheet of cardboard with colorful adhesive-backed paper (or glue on some wrapping paper).

2 Turn over the cardboard. On the side without the paper covering, draw straight lines dividing the cardboard into squares. Cut the squares apart to make cards.

3 Cut out matching pictures from brochures or draw identical pairs of pictures yourself.

4 Glue each picture onto the plain side of a card. Make as many pairs of pictures as you like. The more cards you have, the harder the game will be.

★How to Play★
Lay the cards facedown. Taking turns, each player turns over two cards at a time. If the cards match, the player wins them and can take another turn. When all the cards are gone, the player with the most cards wins!

Sack o' Jacks

Paint peanuts or pieces of pasta to make this toss-and-catch game!

You Will Need

- paints
- paintbrush
- peanuts or bow-tie pasta
- scissors
- felt
- large needle
- embroidery floss or yarn

1 To make the jacks, paint peanuts or pieces of bow-tie pasta with bright colors and let them dry.

2 To make the sack, cut two rectangles out of felt. Lay them together, one on top of the other. Thread a large needle with embroidery floss or yarn. Knot the end of the floss or yarn.

3 Start sewing along one long edge of the felt (as shown) and continue around until the felt pieces are stitched together on three sides. Knot the floss or yarn.

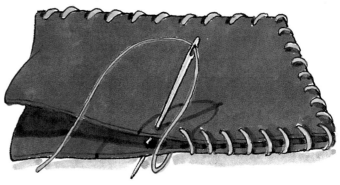

4 Make long stitches around the neck of the sack through only one layer of felt. Knot the ends of the floss or yarn at one side.

5 Thread the needle again and, starting at the opposite side, sew back over the long stitches. Knot the floss or yarn at the other side. The sack now has two drawstrings.

★How to Play★

Toss six jacks into the air. Catch as many as you can on the back of your hand. Then toss those jacks and catch them in your palm. Toss these jacks and pick up one dropped jack before you catch them again. Repeat this series of tossing and catching until you have all the jacks in your hand. You'll improve with practice!

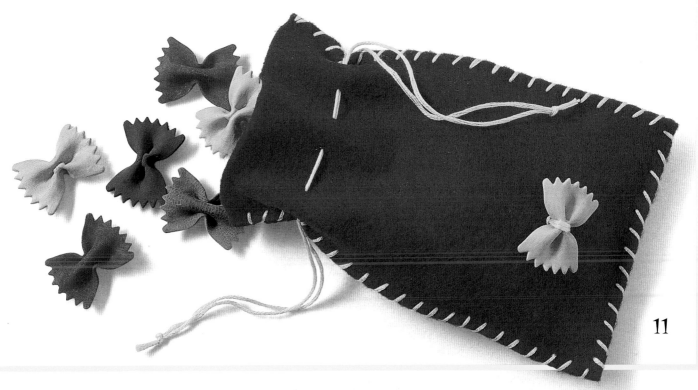

Pup-Pets

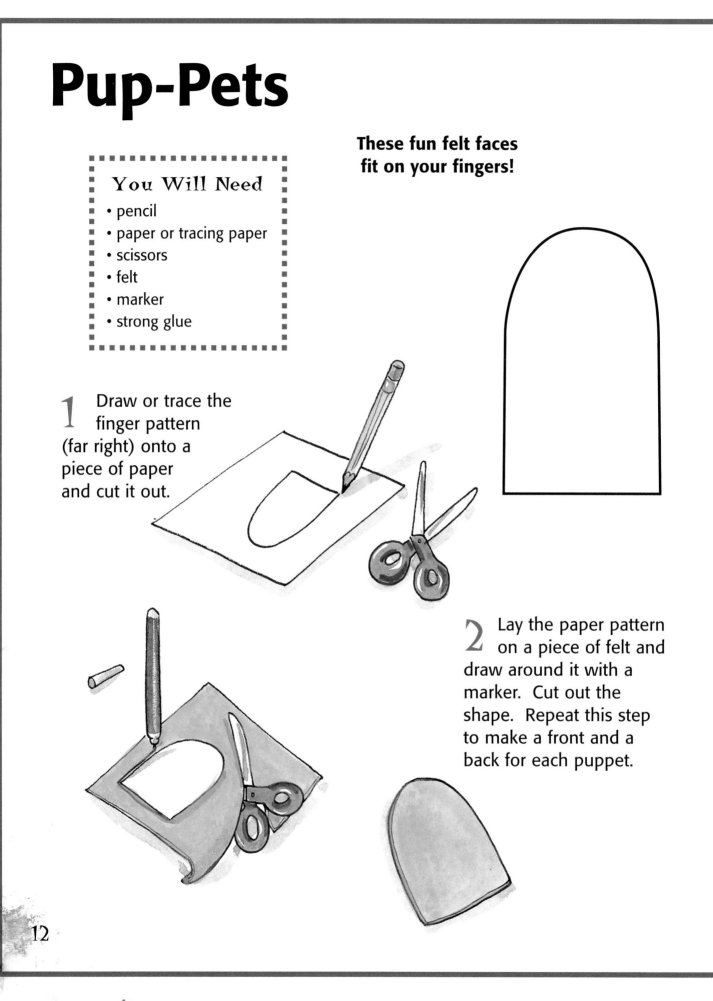

These fun felt faces fit on your fingers!

1 Draw or trace the finger pattern (far right) onto a piece of paper and cut it out.

2 Lay the paper pattern on a piece of felt and draw around it with a marker. Cut out the shape. Repeat this step to make a front and a back for each puppet.

12

3 Cut scraps of felt to make eyes, noses, hair, wings, and other features.

4 Glue the features onto the front pieces of felt. Glue any ears, tails, or wings onto the back sides of the front pieces.

5 Spread a line of glue along the curved edge of the back pieces of felt. Lay the front and back pieces together, with the insides facing, and press them flat.

★ **Bright Idea** ★
Put on a Pup-Pet show for your family and friends!

13

Fortune Teller

**Can you see into the future?
It's fun to pretend. Forecast
good luck for your friends!**

You Will Need
• paper square
• crayons
• pen

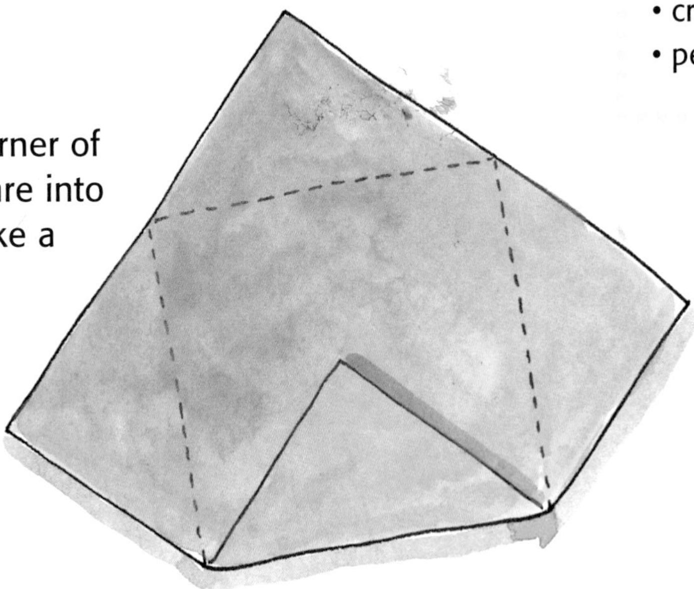

1 Fold each corner of
a paper square into
the center to make a
smaller square.

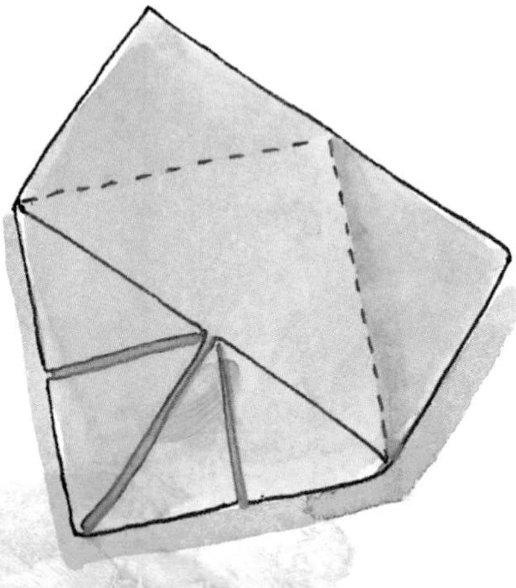

2 Turn the square over and
fold each corner into the
center again.

3 Mark each small triangle
with a crayon dot of a
different color (as shown).

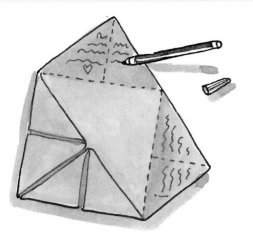

4 Under each flap, write two silly fortunes, such as "You will be the first person on Mars." Write one fortune in each half of the space. There is room for eight fortunes.

5 Turn over the fortune teller and write a number on each of the four flaps.

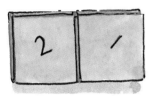

6 Fold the fortune teller in half, unfold it, then fold it in half the other way. Put your thumbs and index fingers inside the numbered flaps.

★How to Play★

Ask a friend to choose a number. Move the fortune teller in and out with your thumbs and fingers as you count to that number. Let your friend choose a colored dot, then lift that flap to reveal the future!

Pickup Sticks

**See if you can snatch
a single stick without
disturbing the rest!**

1 Decorate 30 ice cream sticks with bright paints or markers.

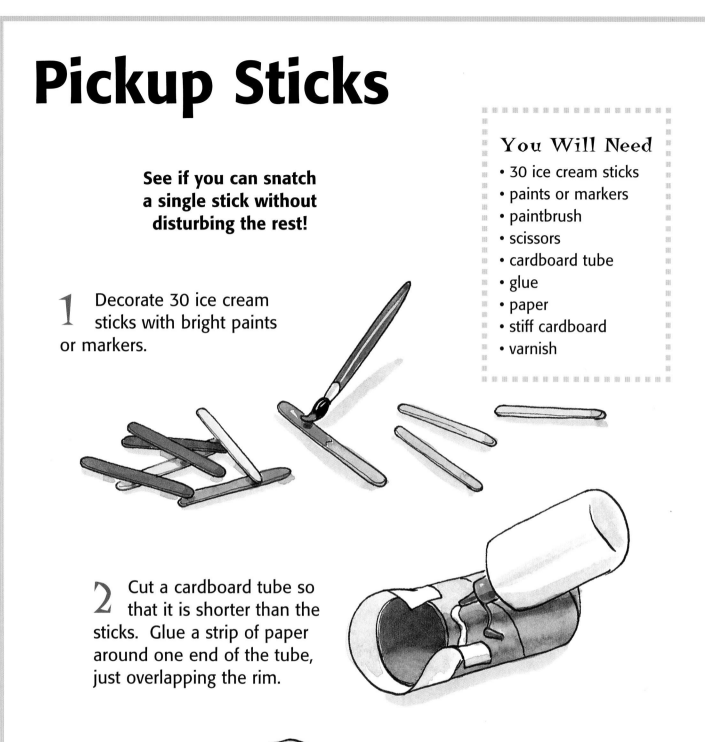

2 Cut a cardboard tube so that it is shorter than the sticks. Glue a strip of paper around one end of the tube, just overlapping the rim.

3 Make a series of evenly spaced cuts into the paper, cutting right up to the rim of the tube.

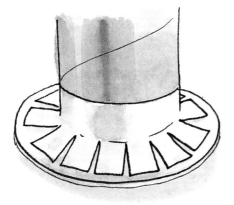

4 Cut out a cardboard circle that is larger around than the tube. Fold out the paper tabs on the tube and glue them flat onto the circle.

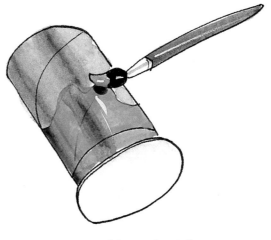

5 Paint both the tube and the cardboard base. When the paint is dry, brush on a coat of varnish.

★How to Play★

Keep one stick to lift with and drop the other sticks in a heap. Each player takes turns using the lifting stick to remove other sticks, one at a time. If a player moves any sticks, except the one being removed, the lifting stick passes to the next player.

Parachutes

Toss this toy high into the sky, then watch it slowly drift back down.

1 Make a small figure out of clay. Push a loop of wire into the top of the figure. Ask an adult to bake the figure in the oven, following the instructions on the package of clay.

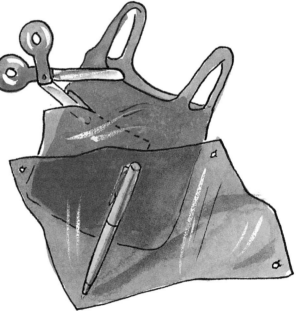

2 Cut a square piece out of a plastic bag. Use a pen to poke a small hole at each corner.

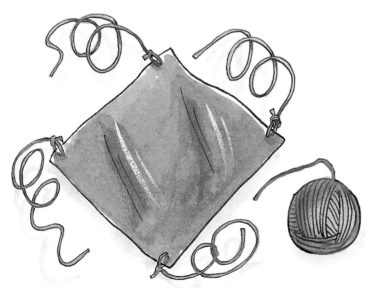

3 Cut four pieces of string that are all the same length. Tie one piece of string to each corner of the plastic square.

18

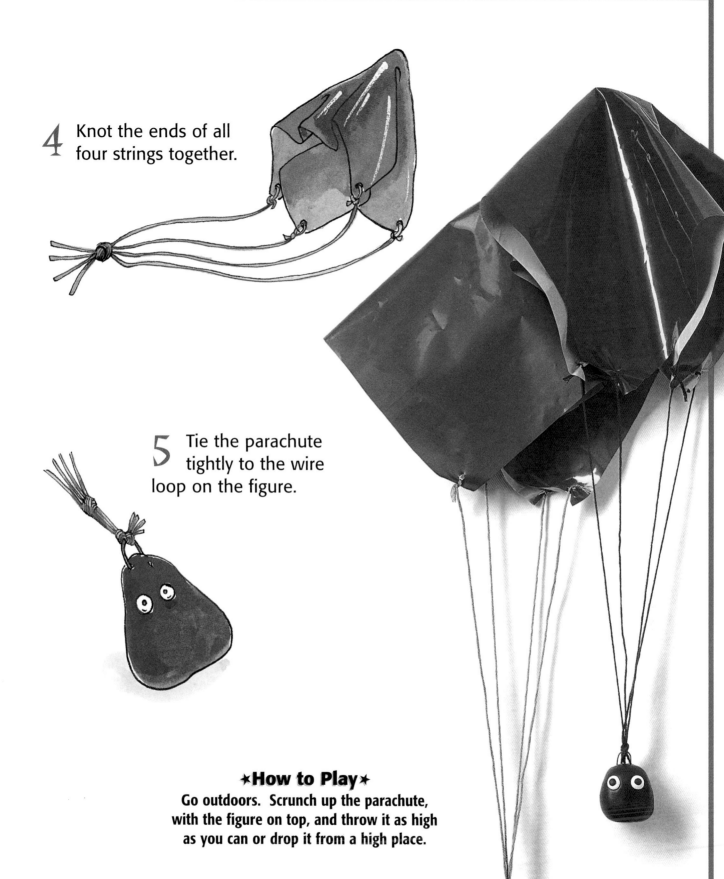

4 Knot the ends of all four strings together.

5 Tie the parachute tightly to the wire loop on the figure.

★**How to Play**★
Go outdoors. Scrunch up the parachute, with the figure on top, and throw it as high as you can or drop it from a high place.

19

Kaleidoscope

**Look toward a light
and turn the tube to view
an ever-changing pattern of color!**

1 Ask an adult to cut a heavy cardboard tube to 7 inches (18 centimeters) long, then cut another piece that is 1/4 inch (6 millimeters) long. Line the inside of the long tube with a rolled-up rectangle of black paper.

2 Cut a rectangle of acetate 7 inches (18 cm) long and about 2 1/2 times the diameter of the cardboard tube. Score the acetate with two lines, dividing the sheet into three equal parts. Fold the acetate along the lines to make a triangular tube. Put the acetate tube inside the cardboard tube.

3 Trace around the end of the cardboard tube on a piece of cardboard and cut out the circle. Poke a peephole in the center of the circle and tape the circle onto one end of the cardboard tube.

4 Cut two acetate disks with the same diameter as the cardboard tube. Place one disk on the open end of the tube and put the cardboard ring on top of it. Tape the ring securely to the tube.

5 Put a handful of beads, paper clips, and other small, colorful shapes into the ring. Tape the other acetate disk over the end of the ring.

6 Decorate your kaleidoscope with paints, markers, or bright wrapping paper.

★ **Bright Idea** ★
Add shiny sequins or glitter to your bits and pieces to reflect more light!

Boat Races

Launch this boat in the sink or float a fleet in the tub!

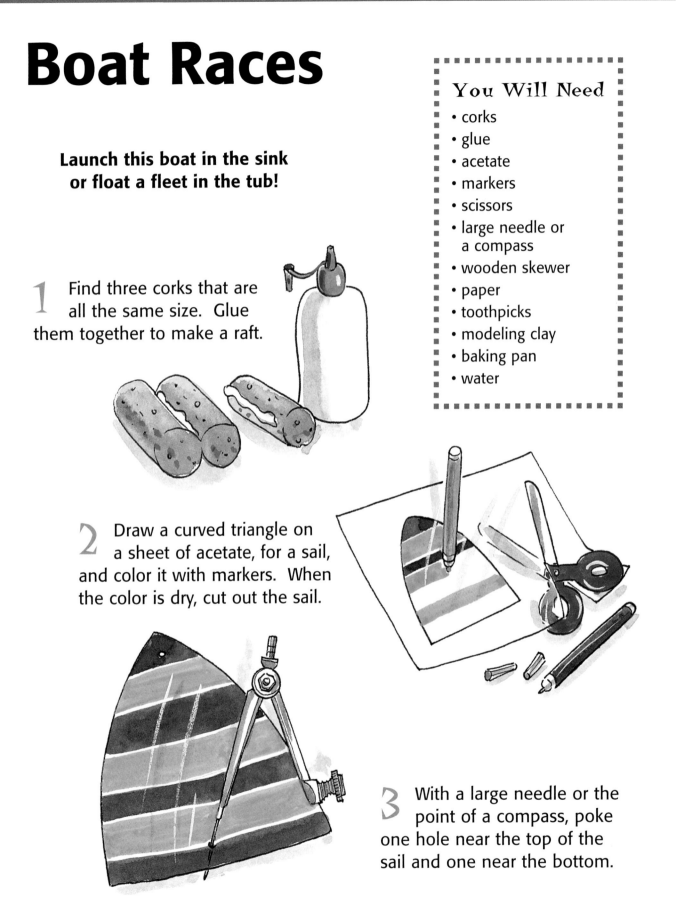

1 Find three corks that are all the same size. Glue them together to make a raft.

2 Draw a curved triangle on a sheet of acetate, for a sail, and color it with markers. When the color is dry, cut out the sail.

3 With a large needle or the point of a compass, poke one hole near the top of the sail and one near the bottom.

4 Push a wooden skewer through the two holes and into the middle cork. Cut the skewer above the sail, if necessary.

5 Cut small flags out of acetate or paper. Stick toothpicks through them and push the toothpicks into small lumps of clay. Arrange the flags in a large baking pan and add water.

★How to Play★

Blow your boat around the racing course with a straw. Race two boats together, or time each boat as it completes the course separately.

Bead Boy

String a jiggly figure that can stretch and bounce and dance!

You Will Need
- elastic string
- 6 small beads
- 12 long beads
- 6 big round beads
- scissors

1 On a long piece of elastic string, thread one small bead, three long beads, and another small bead. Bring the string back through the three long beads.

2 Thread on two big round beads, three long beads, and one small bead. Bring the string back through the three long beads.

3 Thread on one big round bead, three long beads, and one small bead. Bring the string back through the three long beads.

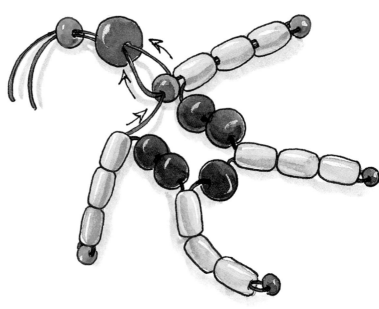

4 Repeat step 2, then bring the string back through the small bead you started with. Thread both ends of the string through one big round bead and one small bead.

5 Adjust the beads so the tension on the elastic string is even. Tie a knot just above the top bead and tie another knot higher up. Trim off the ends of the string.

★ Bright Idea ★
Experiment with bead shapes and sizes to make all kinds of different bead people!

Jugglers

Toss them and catch them, again and again! The trick is to keep them in motion.

You Will Need
- scissors
- felt
- ruler
- marker
- thread
- large needle
- dry beans

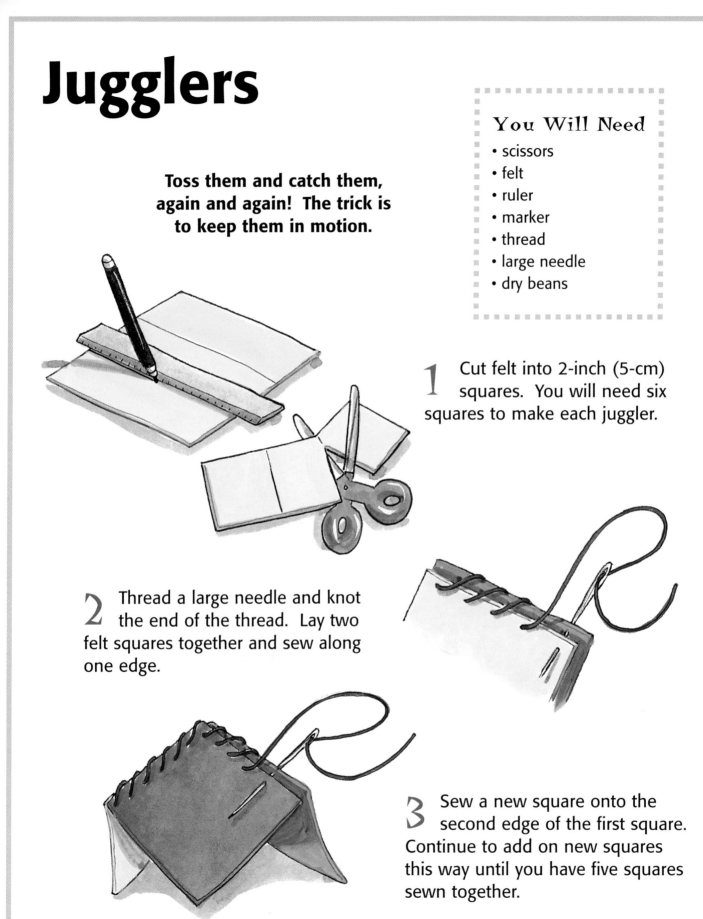

1 Cut felt into 2-inch (5-cm) squares. You will need six squares to make each juggler.

2 Thread a large needle and knot the end of the thread. Lay two felt squares together and sew along one edge.

3 Sew a new square onto the second edge of the first square. Continue to add on new squares this way until you have five squares sewn together.

4 Sew all the sides of the squares together to form a box. Sew on the sixth square, like a lid, but leave a gap along one side.

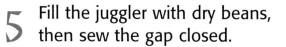

5 Fill the juggler with dry beans, then sew the gap closed.

★How to Play★

Start with one juggler. Practice tossing it from hand to hand, without watching. To toss three jugglers, throw them in a crisscross pattern.

Flip-a-Coin

**Test your skill on the stripes.
Every color counts!**

You Will Need

• scissors
• shoe box with a lid
• pencil
• coin
• markers
• white cardboard
• beans or counters

1   Cut the flap off of one narrow
    end on the lid of a shoe box.

2   Use a narrow end on the
    bottom of the box to draw
seven pencil lines across the
inside of the lid. The distance
between each line should be
just a little more than the size
of the coin you will use to play
the game.

3 Color in the stripes on the lid with markers, but leave the far end of the lid blank.

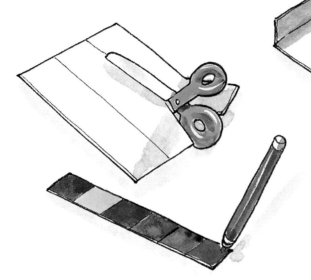

4 Cut a strip of cardboard for each player to keep score on. Color the cardboard strips to exactly match the stripes on the playing board.

★How to Play★

Place a coin at the edge of the board and hit it with a flat hand. The coin must land on each color three times. Keep score by placing a bean or a counter on your cardboard strip for each successful landing.

29

Sticky Ball

Catch a ball with a mitt that won't let go!

1 Place your catching hand facedown on a plastic or paper plate. Mark both sides of your hand. Ask an adult to cut a slot along each mark with a craft knife.

2 Thread wide ribbon or cloth tape through the slots to make a handle on the back of the plate. Check that your hand fits, then glue the ends of the ribbon or tape to the inside of the plate.

3 Stick Velcro dots (the rough side) over the ends of the ribbon or tape and around the inside of the plate.

4 Paint a Styrofoam ball. When the paint is dry, stick Velcro dots (the furry side) evenly around the ball.

★**How to Play**★
Team up with a friend. Toss the furry ball back and forth and catch it with your sticky mitts.

31

Snap!

**Keep an eye on the cards
and be ready to SNAP!**

You Will Need
- white cardboard
- colored markers
- pencil
- ruler
- scissors
- black marker

1 On a large sheet of white cardboard, draw shapes with markers.

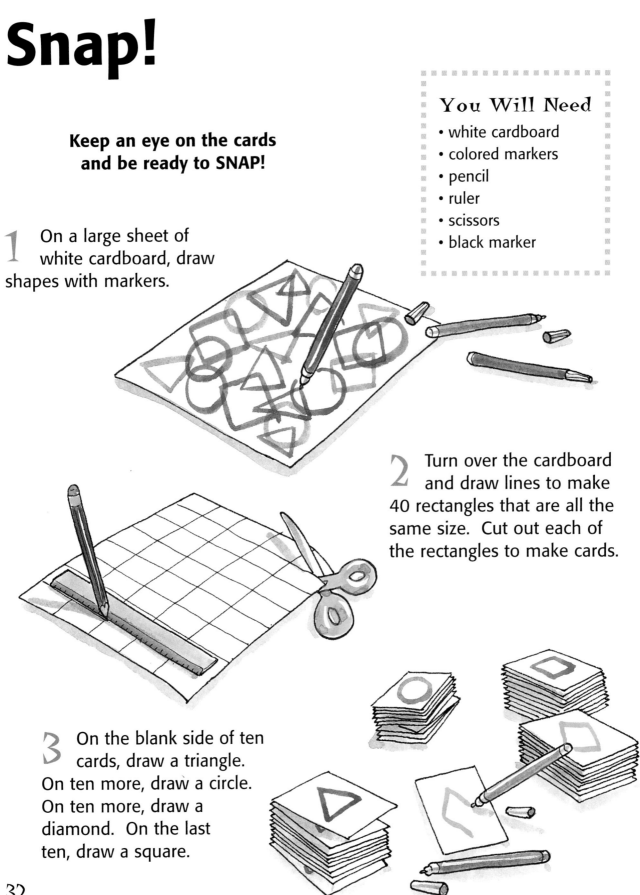

2 Turn over the cardboard and draw lines to make 40 rectangles that are all the same size. Cut out each of the rectangles to make cards.

3 On the blank side of ten cards, draw a triangle. On ten more, draw a circle. On ten more, draw a diamond. On the last ten, draw a square.

4 On two triangle cards, write the number *1* with a black marker. On two more, write the number *2*. Continue writing numbers, up to 5, on every two triangle cards.

5 Repeat step 4 for the circle cards, the diamond cards, and the square cards.

★How to Play★

Divide the cards among the players. Take turns turning a card faceup on a pile. When two cards with the same number and shape appear one after the other, the first player to shout "Snap!" wins the pile. The game ends when one player has all the cards.

Flying Trapeze

All it takes is a tap to make these fearless high flyers flip and spin.

You Will Need
- tracing paper
- pencil
- thin white cardboard
- scissors
- markers
- glue
- 2 small coins
- drinking straw
- string
- tape

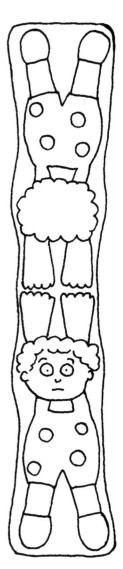

1 Trace over the pattern (right) in pencil. Lay the tracing facedown on cardboard and draw over the lines. Cut out the cardboard figure along the pencil outline.

2 Repeat step 1 to make a second figure, then color both figures with markers.

3 On the back of one figure, glue a small coin at each end. Cut off a piece of a drinking straw and glue it in the middle of the same figure. Glue the other figure on top.

34

4 Thread string through the piece of straw. Cut two long strips of cardboard. Tape each end of the string to the middle of a cardboard strip (as shown).

5 Fold each strip in half and bend back the ends to make two flaps.

6 Glue the insides of the strips and color the outsides. Cut a piece of cardboard for a base. Glue the flaps onto it so the strips are standing up and are far enough apart that the figure does not touch the base.

★How to Play★
Give these acrobats a light push and watch them perform!

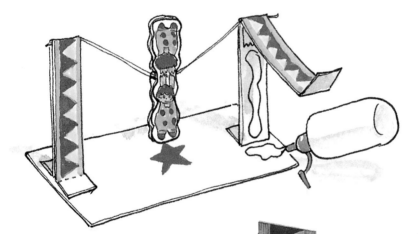

35

Snakes 'n' Ladders

Climb way up and slide back down in this classic game of chance!

1 Draw eighteen squares on one color of paper and another eighteen squares on a different color of paper. Cut out all of the squares.

2 Arrange the squares on stiff cardboard in a checkerboard pattern with six rows. Glue each square in place.

3 Starting at the bottom left corner, number each square, from 1 to 36. At the end of each row, work up and then sideways.

4 Cut pipe cleaners to different lengths and bend them into snakes. Twist one end into a circle, for a head, and glue on paper eyes.

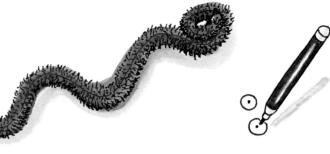

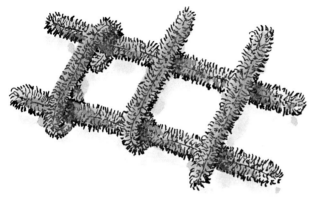

5 Cut two long pieces of pipe cleaner and join them with several short pieces to make a ladder. Make more ladders of different lengths. Arrange the ladders and the snakes on the numbered playing board.

6 Make a spinner. (See page 7 for instructions.)

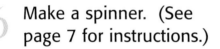

★ How to Play ★

Take turns spinning and moving game pieces around the board, following the numbered squares. When you land at the bottom of a ladder, climb to the top. When you land on a snake's head, slide back down. The first player to reach square 36 wins!

37

Whirligigs

Send these fabulous flyers flipping and fluttering through the air!

You Will Need

- ruler
- scissors
- corrugated cardboard
- paint and paintbrush
- glue
- colored paper
- pencil
- modeling clay
- thin cardboard
- tape

1 Measure and cut a strip of corrugated cardboard that is 8 inches by 1 inch (20 cm by 2.5 cm). Paint both sides or glue on some bright colored paper.

2 Round the corners of the cardboard strip with scissors to form a propeller. Mark the center of the propeller and, with the tip of a scissors, carefully poke a hole that the propeller shaft will fit into tightly.

3 Glue paper around a pencil. Spread glue around the tip of the pencil and push the tip into the hole in the propeller. Put a small ball of clay on the pencil tip.

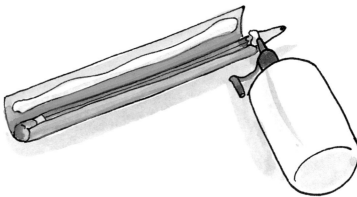

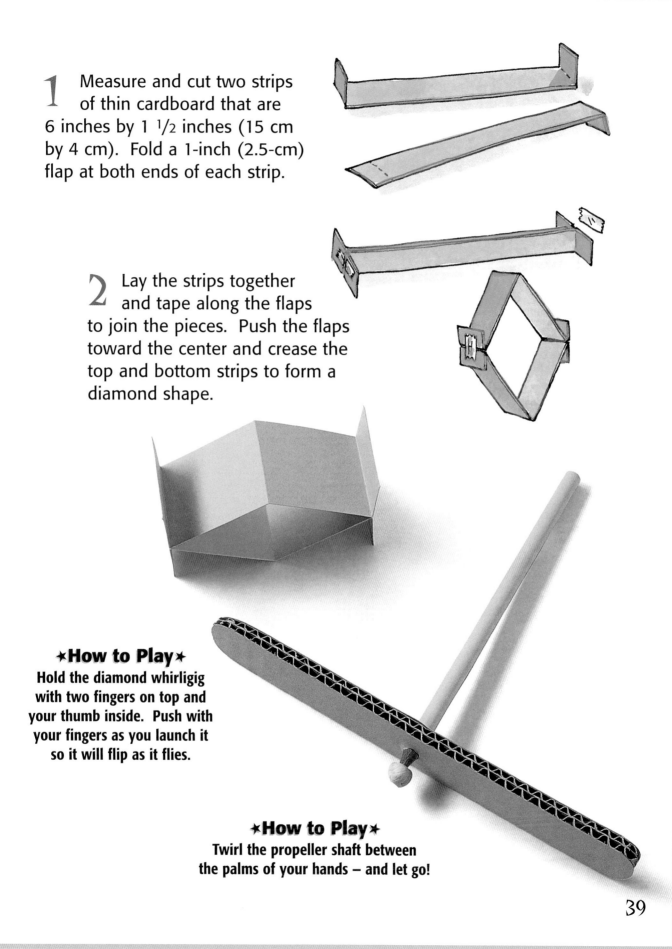

1 Measure and cut two strips of thin cardboard that are 6 inches by 1 ½ inches (15 cm by 4 cm). Fold a 1-inch (2.5-cm) flap at both ends of each strip.

2 Lay the strips together and tape along the flaps to join the pieces. Push the flaps toward the center and crease the top and bottom strips to form a diamond shape.

★**How to Play**★
Hold the diamond whirligig with two fingers on top and your thumb inside. Push with your fingers as you launch it so it will flip as it flies.

★**How to Play**★
Twirl the propeller shaft between the palms of your hands – and let go!

39

Bottle Bowling

Ready! Aim! Bowl over these striped pins with a sock!

1 Wash out and dry three plastic bottles. Pour a few handfuls of dry sand into each bottle.

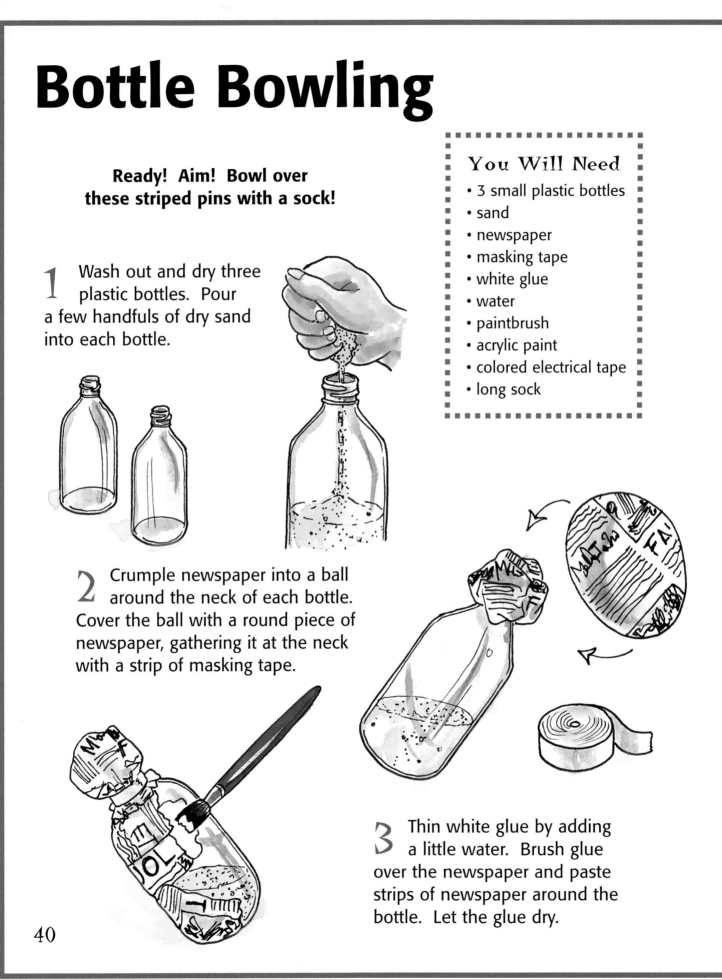

2 Crumple newspaper into a ball around the neck of each bottle. Cover the ball with a round piece of newspaper, gathering it at the neck with a strip of masking tape.

3 Thin white glue by adding a little water. Brush glue over the newspaper and paste strips of newspaper around the bottle. Let the glue dry.

40

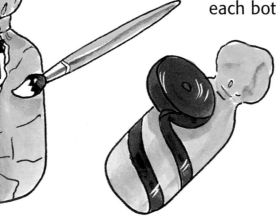

4 Paint the bottles. When the paint is dry, wind colored electrical tape around each bottle in a spiral design.

5 Make a sock ball by twisting the toe of a long sock and pulling the rest of the sock over the toe. Keep twisting and pulling until the sock is all rolled up.

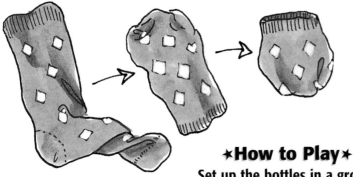

★How to Play★
Set up the bottles in a group.
See how many you can bowl
over with the sock ball.

41

Buzzers

**Wind it up and let it spin.
Listen to it hum!**

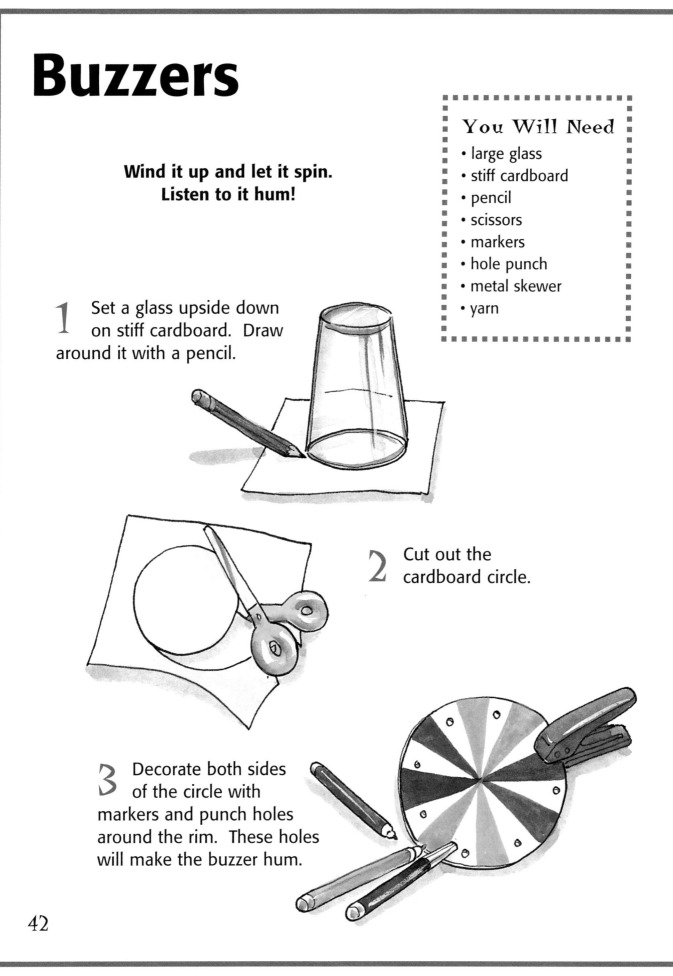

1 Set a glass upside down on stiff cardboard. Draw around it with a pencil.

2 Cut out the cardboard circle.

3 Decorate both sides of the circle with markers and punch holes around the rim. These holes will make the buzzer hum.

4 With a metal skewer or the point of a scissors, poke two holes in the circle, one on each side of the center. Make each hole the same distance from the center.

5 Cut a long piece of yarn. Thread the yarn through the skewer holes and tie the ends together.

★How to Play★
Turn the buzzer many times in the same direction to wind it up. Then pull the yarn and watch it twirl!

Blow Ball

You Will Need

- paint
- paintbrush
- cardboard tubes
- 8 matchboxes
- colored paper
- scissors
- string or rope
- glue
- Ping-Pong ball
- drinking straws

Score a goal without touching the ball!

1 Paint cardboard tubes and matchboxes or cover them with colored paper.

2 Cut a piece of string or rope long enough to fit around a table. Thread the string or rope through all of the cardboard tubes.

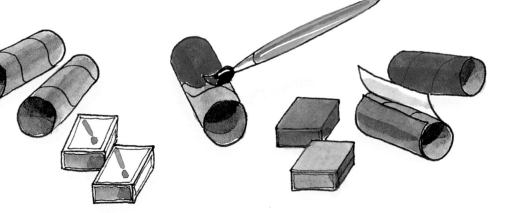

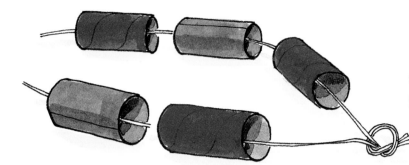

3 Tie the ends of the string or rope together. Arrange the tubes around a table to form a boundary.

4 Glue together four matchboxes (as shown) to make a goal. Make a second goal the same way. Place one goal at each end of the table, inside the boundary.

★How to Play★
Place a Ping-Pong ball in the center of the table. Try to score a goal by blowing on the ball through a straw.

Twist-a-Beast

**Combine the features of
three different creatures to
make some amazing new animals!**

1 Ask an adult to cut a cardboard tube with a craft knife to make the tube 4 1/2 inches (11.5 cm) long. Cut two strips of cardboard, each 3/8 inch (1 cm) wide, to fit around the tube. Color the strips with a marker.

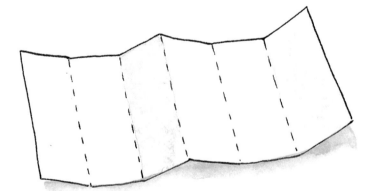

2 Cut a piece of paper 3 1/2 inches (9 cm) wide and 3/4 inch (2 cm) longer than the cardboard strips. Fold the paper into six equal panels.

3 Check the fit of the paper around the tube. All sides should touch the tube, and the ends of the paper should meet. Adjust the size, if necessary.

4 Use the paper as a pattern to cut a piece of cardboard. Have an adult score lightly along the fold lines. Remove the paper and draw two lines to divide the cardboard panels into three sections.

5 Draw an animal on each panel of the cardboard. Color the animals. Cut along the dividing lines to make three strips. Tape each strip into a ring.

6 Glue a colored cardboard strip around the bottom of the tube. Slip on the three animal rings, in order. Glue the other cardboard strip around the top of the tube.

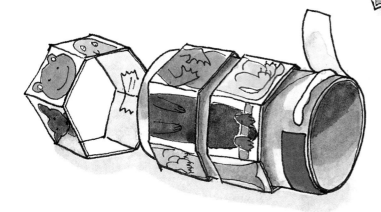

★How to Play★
Turn the rings in different directions to view your zany zoo!

47

Glossary

acetate: a type of plastic that comes in thin, flexible sheets that are clear, or transparent.

adhesive-backed: having a sticky coating on the back side.

compass: a tool for drawing circles, which has two arms, one with a sharp point and one that holds a pencil.

corrugated: having a wrinkled surface or a surface of ridges and grooves.

hexagon: a shape with six sides and six angles.

identical: exactly the same.

kaleidoscope: a tube that is held up to the eye and twisted to form changing patterns as the result of mirrors reflecting bits of colored glass.

overlapping: lying over the top of something and partly covering it.

score: to cut or scratch lines or grooves into a surface without cutting all the way through.

skewer: a long, pointed, wooden or metal pin, used to hold food together while it is cooking.

Styrofoam: the trademark name for a light-weight, foamlike plastic.

Velcro: the trademark name for a nylon material that fastens items together when tiny hooks on one side are pressed against softer loops on the other side.

whirligigs: toys that continuously turn or spin when air pushes against them.

More Craft Books by Gareth Stevens

Crafty Juggling. Crafty Kids (series).
  Nick Huckleberry Beak

Crafty Puppets. Crafty Kids (series).
  Thomasina Smith

Kids Create! Williamson Kids Can!® (series).
  Laurie Carlson

Perfect Parties. Handy Crafts (series).
  Gillian Souter

Index